SACRED CODE

UNLOCKING LIFE CHANGING LAWS

SACHIN GAUTAM

To my parents,
For your unwavering love and support. Your presence kept
me grounded throughout the writing of this book.

To my mentor,
Your guidance shaped my personality and brought clarity
to my path. Without you, this book wouldn't exist.

To my friends,
Thank you for challenging my ideas and pushing me to
grow. Your criticism was a gift that helped me improve.

Contents

Contents

FOREWORD

"What lies behind us and what lies before us are tiny matters compared to what lies within us."
-Ralph Waldo Emerson

In every era , a few voices rise to remind us that science is not just a discipline of the mind- it is an expression of wonder. Sacred code is one such voice, and it belongs to my student, Sachin.

It is with deep pride and immense joy that i introduce Sacred code , a groundbreaking work by my student, Sachin. It is rare to find a book that shows together threads from so many dimensions- science, spirit, tradition, and transformation- with such clarity and grace. Each chapter is not just an offering of knolwedge but an invitation to remembrance.

Grounding, sun salutation, Tratak,Vipassana , the Art of self mastery- These are not only practices; they are portals to a deeper understanding of what is means to be humans.

Sachin's mind doesn't rest at the surface. He is drawn to what lies beneath, what pulses behind the obvious. And in Sacred code, he brings that gift to all of us. This book is the result of years of inquiry, not only into scientific literature , but into the deeper currents of life itself.

Let this book guide you not only to new knowledge, but to inner knowing. Let it remind you that beneath all complexity , life is not noise- it is a music. A symphony. And we are each a note in its divine composition.

I believe this book will find its way into the hands of those who are ready to rewire their understanding of reality- not through theory alone, but through practice presence, and embodiment.

With heartful blessings,
Murali Chavala

PREFACE

In my Teenage era, I found myself stuck in a state of low productivity, poor health, and dull cognition. Searching for a way out, I came across universal laws that sparked my journey of truth-seeking.

My curiosity about the universe led me to The Secret, which offered hope—even if I couldn't fully grasp it then. After a couple of unproductive years lost in thought, I realized the need for real action. That's when I discovered Prashant Trivedi, whose teachings on posture and purposeful living brought clarity and direction.

This book shares the key laws and techniques I've learned—tools that can help you align with nature, take control of your life, and invite better health, luck, and understanding.

It all begins with right thinking and right action.

Prologue

Bioelectricity is the subtle energy that powers every cell in our body. It is this natural electrical force that keeps our heart beating, our brain working, and helps the body heal itself. In ancient Indian texts, this energy is known as Prana, and in other cultures, it is called Chi. It controls all functions of the body—physical, mental, emotional, and even spiritual. The more of this energy you have, the healthier and stronger you feel.

But bioelectricity is not just about the body. It also connects the mind and spirit. It is the invisible link that brings balance and awareness to our whole being.

Ancient Indian traditions have always understood this. Practices like yoga, meditation, pranayama, and proper breathing were never just for relaxation. They are powerful tools to increase and balance your inner energy. When used correctly, they can bring big changes in your life.

Modern science is slowly starting to accept this idea. While it's hard to prove directly, method like Kirlian photography shows that we do have an energy field around us. When this energy field becomes strong, it protects and empowers us.

This book is about discovering that power within you.

From connecting to the Earth's natural energy to practicing self-discipline, from doing Trataka, Vipassana, and Surya Namaskar, to understanding nature's laws, the power of gratitude, energy infections, and the heart-brain connection—each chapter will guide you towards a better, more balanced life.

You will also learn how simple things like your posture, the way you speak, and your facial expressions affect your energy and your reality. By following spiritual values and living with awareness, you can tune your energy with the rhythm of life.

As you read this book, I hope you don't just understand these ideas—but feel them. May you find clarity, peace, and strength. Because when your inner energy flows properly, life becomes joyful, clear, and full of meaning.

I
Grounding

In today's fast running world, many of us have become energetically disconnected—from nature and from ourselves. Grounding, also known as earthing, is the practice of consciously reconnecting with the Earth's subtle energy. While it was popularized by Clint Ober in the 1990s, the concept has ancient roots in various cultures. It is a simple yet powerful tool to restore balance, reduce stress, and bring clarity to the mind and stability to the body.

The Science and Spirituality of Grounding

At a biological level, our bodies carry a natural electrical charge. The Earth, too, has its own stable, negative charge, which is maintained by a constant flow of electrons. When we make direct contact with the Earth—by walking barefoot on soil, grass, sand, or stone—free electrons flow into the body, neutralizing harmful free radicals and reducing inflammation.

Spiritually, grounding is the act of anchoring our awareness into the present moment. It allows us to shift from chaotic thought patterns into a state of peace. Ancient traditions have always emphasized our connection to the Earth as a source of healing, stability, and intuitive wisdom. Grounding aligns the root chakra (Muladhara), our energetic foundation, which governs survival, safety, and trust.

Benefits of Grounding

- <u>Emotional Balance</u>: Helps in calming anxiety, anger, and emotional reactivity by stabilizing the nervous system.
- <u>Physical Vitality</u>: Reduces chronic pain and inflammation, improves sleep, and supports immune function.
- <u>Mental Clarity</u>: Grounds scattered thoughts, improves focus, and encourages practical decision making.
- <u>Energetic Stability</u>: Recharges the body's bioelectric field, aligning it with the Earth's frequency.
- <u>Spiritual Alignment</u>: Enhances your ability to remain present during meditation or prayer, fostering deeper connection to self and Source.

Simple Grounding Practices

1. Barefoot Walking: Spend at least 10–20 minutes a day walking barefoot on natural surfaces such as grass, soil, or sand.

2. Tree Connection: Sit beneath a tree or rest your hand on its trunk. Visualize drawing strength and steadiness from its deep roots.

3. Visualization Technique: Sit or lie down. Close your eyes and imagine roots growing from the base of your spine or feet into the Earth. Feel yourself anchored, supported, and nourished by the planet.

4. Breath Awareness: Inhale deeply through the nose, feeling the breath travel down to your belly. Exhale slowly and visualize releasing all excess energy into the Earth.

Grounding and the Root Chakra

Grounding practices awaken and balance the root chakra, our energetic center of survival and belonging. When this chakra is underactive, we may feel fearful, insecure, or disoriented. When balanced, it brings stability, discipline, and trust in life. Grounding rituals serve as a daily reminder that we are safe, supported, and connected.

Signs You Need Grounding :

- Feeling mentally scattered or overly emotional
- Experiencing insomnia or chronic fatigue
- Frequent worry or anxiety
- Forgetfulness and lack of presence
- Being overly reactive or unbalanced in communication

Conclusion

Grounding is not just a physical act—it is a spiritual return to our natural state of harmony. In grounding, we remember that we are not separate from the Earth, but of it. We rediscover our center, our strength, and our stillness. In a world that pulls us upward into the chaos of the mind and digital distractions, grounding brings us downward—into the body, into the breath, and into the heart of the living Earth. Reconnect with the ground beneath your feet, and you will find the peace that cannot be shaken.

II

Sun Salutation and The EBBC Namaste Technique

In yogic tradition, the Sun Salutation (Surya Namaskar) is more than a physical sequence—it is a moving prayer, an offering to the solar energy within and around us. Complementing this is the EBBC Namaste Technique, a mindful method of salutation and energetic connection from the Energy Way tradition, used to consciously align body, breath, and presence.

Together, these practices form a gateway into inner awakening, balances masculine and feminine energy within guiding the practitioner to harmonize movement, breath, intention, and energy.

Part I :Sun Salutation

"Surya" means Sun, and "Namaskar" means to bow or salute. This ancient sequence of twelve movements is designed to energize the body, calm the mind, and honor the life-giving force of the Sun—both external and internal.

Each pose is paired with a specific breath, creating a rhythm that balances solar (masculine, active) and lunar (feminine, receptive) energies.

Benefits of Surya Namaskar

- Physical: Enhances flexibility, improves circulation, tones muscles, and supports cardiovascular health.
- Mental: Increases focus, reduces anxiety, and enhances emotional resilience.
- Energetic: Activates the solar plexus (Manipura chakra), which governs personal power and inner fire.
- Spiritual: Fosters devotion, surrender, and alignment with natural cycles

The 12 Steps of Sun Salutation

1. Pranamasana (Prayer Pose) – Inhale
2. Hasta Uttanasana (Raised Arms Pose) – Exhale
3. Padahastasana (Standing Forward Bend) – Inhale
4. Ashwa Sanchalanasana (Equestrian Pose) – Exhale
5. Dandasana (Plank Pose) – Inhale
6. Ashtanga Namaskara (Eight-Point Pose) – Exhale
7. Bhujangasana (Cobra Pose) – Inhale
8. Adho Mukha Svanasana (Downward Dog) – Exhale
9. Ashwa Sanchalanasana (Repeat Left Leg) – Inhale
10. Padahastasana (Standing Forward Bend) – Exhale

11. Hasta Uttanasana (Raised Arms Pose) – Inhale
12. Pranamasana (Prayer Pose) – Exhale

Part II: The EBBC Namaste Technique

EBBC stands for Energy – Building – Brain – Connection.

This approach to Namaste transforms a simple greeting into a conscious act of energetic alignment. Rooted in Energy Way philosophy, this technique encourages presence, energetic resonance, and heartfelt connection—whether directed toward oneself, another, or the universe.

The four pillar of EBBC:

Step 1: Join Your Hands Line by Line

Begin by bringing your palms together in a prayer position at your sternum. Pressing your palms together gently, feel the alignment and balance this creates in your body.

Step 2: Smile and Stretch Your Lips

As you maintain the hand position, stretch your lips into a broad smile. This not only lifts your mood but also engages facial muscles, promoting relaxation.

Step 3: Feel the Stretch in Your Elbows

While smiling, notice the subtle stretch in your elbows. This sensation indicates the activation of your upper body muscles.

- **Eyes – Soften your gaze.** Whether closed or gently open, bring awareness to the point between the eyebrows (Ajna chakra). This activates inner vision and receptivity.
- **Breath** – Inhale slowly and deeply into the belly. Exhale with awareness. This connects you to the life force (prana) and brings the nervous system into balance.
- **Body** – Stand or sit with an aligned spine. Bring palms together in front of the heart. Feel the connection between your feet and the Earth, your head and the sky.
- **Consciousness** – With full presence, silently or aloud say Namaste—meaning "The Divine in me honors the Divine in you." Visualize energy flowing from your heart to the person or space you're greeting.

Uses of the EBBC Namaste

- As a morning ritual before or after Surya Namaskar
- Before meditation, healing sessions, or important conversations
- As a way to center yourself in public or chaotic spaces
- To bring awareness and reverence to daily interactions

Integrating Sun Salutation and EBBC Namaste

Start your day by standing in stillness and performing the EBBC Namaste, setting a clear intention. Then move into the flowing sequence of Surya Namaskar. After completing your cycles, return to stillness and repeat the EBBC Namaste with renewed awareness.

This sequence not only awakens your body but aligns your energy with the solar intelligence of the universe. It reminds you that every breath, every gesture, every greeting can be a conscious offering to the divine rhythm of life.

Conclusion

In honoring the Sun and greeting life with awareness, you awaken the sacred within. The Sun Salutation energizes your being, while the EBBC Namaste grounds you in presence. Together, they create a spiritual handshake between your body and the cosmos.

Start with reverence, move with intention, and close with gratitude. This is the way of the awakened being.

III

The Art of Self-Mastery : Yogic Discipline

Self-mastery is the conscious cultivation of one's physical, mental, and spiritual faculties to achieve optimal well-being and purpose. Frank Rudolph Young's Yoga for Men Only offers a unique perspective on this journey, emphasizing techniques tailored for men to enhance vitality, confidence, and inner strength. This chapter explores these principles, providing practical guidance for those seeking to harness their inner power.

1. Understanding Self-Mastery

- Physical Discipline: Developing strength, flexibility, and control over bodily functions.

- Mental Clarity: Cultivating focus, resilience, and emotional balance.
- Spiritual Awareness: Connecting with one's inner self and aligning with higher purposes.

Young emphasizes that through dedicated practice, individuals can rejuvenate their bodies, sharpen their minds, and awaken latent potentials.

2. Yogametrics: The Fusion of Yoga and Isometrics

Young introduces "Yogametrics," a system combining yoga postures with isometric exercises to build muscle strength and internal energy

- Dynamic Tension: Engaging muscles without movement to enhance strength.
- Focused Breathing: Synchronizing breath with muscle engagement to amplify energy flow.
- Postural Precision: Maintaining correct alignment to optimize benefits. This approach not only develops physical prowess but also enhances mental concentration and energy control.

3. Breathing Techniques for Energy and Clarity

Breath control is central to self-mastery

- Deep Diaphragmatic Breathing: Inhaling deeply to oxygenate the body and calm the mind.
- Rhythmic Breathing Patterns: Establishing consistent breathing rhythms to stabilize emotions and focus.
- Breath Retention: Holding the breath momentarily to build internal energy and discipline.

4. *Mental Conditioning and Visualization*

- Positive Affirmations: Repeating empowering statements to reinforce self-belief.
- Visualization: Mentally rehearsing desired outcomes to program the subconscious mind.
- Mindfulness Practices: Staying present to enhance awareness and decision-making.

5. *Ethical Living and Purposeful Action*

Self-mastery extends beyond personal development to ethical living:

- Integrity: Aligning actions with values to build trust and self-respect.
- Discipline: Committing to routines and practices that support growth.
- Service: Using one's abilities to contribute positively to others and society.

6. Practical Techniques for Self-Mastery

A. Myo-Pectoral Technique for Instant Confidence

Purpose: To banish fear and instill immediate confidence.

Steps:

1. Sit upright with your torso relaxed.

2. Place your hands, palms down, on your thighs.

3. Rotate your shoulders forward and downward, engaging your pectoral muscles.

4. Hold this contraction briefly while maintaining deep, rhythmic breathing.

5. Release and repeat as needed.

This technique leverages muscle engagement to influence mental states, promoting a sense of control and assurance.

B. Yogametric Dynamic Tension Exercise

Purpose: To build strength and internal energy without movement.

Steps:

1. Stand or sit comfortably with a straight spine.
2. Choose a muscle group (e.g., biceps) and contract it maximally without moving the limb.
3. Maintain the contraction for 5–10 seconds while breathing deeply.
4. Release and rest for a few seconds.
5. Repeat for other muscle groups

This practice enhances muscle tone and energy flow, contributing to overall vitality.

Conclusion

The journey of self-mastery is a holistic endeavor, integrating body, mind, and spirit. Drawing from Young's teachings and yogic traditions, this path offers a structured approach to unlocking one's full potential. Through consistent practice, ethical living, and inner awareness, individuals can transform their lives, achieving balance, strength, and purposeful existence

IV

The Power of Thought

Every thought we entertain and every emotion we experience emits a powerful energetic vibration that extends into the universe. These vibrations, though subtle, shape our reality. Much like tuning forks that resonate with matching frequencies, the energy we project attracts circumstances, individuals, and opportunities that align with our internal state. This principle is not just a modern concept but is mentioned in ancient texts and philosophies. Through personal experience, one can discern the visible impact of this law in shaping one's life. It stands as the fundamental law governing the interplay between consciousness and creation.

1. The Law of Mental Magnetism

Ancient wisdom across cultures has echoed this idea: like attracts like. Our minds are not isolated chambers; they are broadcasting towers, constantly sending out signals. These signals, composed of beliefs, expectations, and emotions, attract circumstances that mirror them.

- Positive thoughts attract growth, abundance, and joy.
- Negative thoughts invite conflict, stagnation, and limitation.
- Mastering our internal dialogue is thus the first step in consciously shaping our life.

2. Feelings: The Compass of Manifestation

Thoughts generate feelings, and feelings are the magnetic forces behind attraction. When we feel joy, gratitude, or love, we align with higher frequencies that invite harmony and abundance. Conversely, feelings of fear, resentment, or lack tune us into lower vibrations.

3. Visualization and Mental Rehearsal

Visualization is a yogic and psychological technique that programs the subconscious mind and aligns your energy field. When you vividly imagine an outcome with full sensory engagement, your nervous system begins to believe it is real.

4. Gratitude

Gratitude is not just a moral virtue—it's a vibrational tool. When you feel thankful, you affirm abundance and invite more of it. It is the simplest yet most profound practice for elevating your state of being

5. Inner Alignment Over Outer Effort

Effort is important, but when action is misaligned with your inner state, it becomes struggle. True power lies in inspired action—steps taken from a place of clarity and enthusiasm.

- Align first: through breath, meditation, or stillness.
- Act next: from flow, not force.
- Let go: of excessive control and allow synchronicities to guide you.

Conclusion

Your mind is the architect of your reality, and your feelings are the builders. By consciously directing your thoughts and emotions, you awaken the innate ability to shape your life in alignment with your highest potential. The universe responds not to what you merely wish for, but to what you truly believe and feel.

As you walk this path, remember: you are not a passive recipient of fate—you are a powerful participant in the cosmic dance of creation.

V

Inner Healer

Within each of us lies an extraordinary power—a silent healer that listens to every thought, feels every belief, and reflects them into the body. Our emotions and inner dialogue do not exist in isolation; they are the seeds from which our physical, mental, and spiritual health grows. Illness and imbalance often begin in the unseen realms of the mind and heart, long before they manifest in the body. Healing, then, is not merely about fixing symptoms—it is about transforming consciousness.

1. The Mind-Body Connection

The body is a mirror of the mind. Every cell, organ, and system responds to the messages we send through our thoughts and emotions. Fear contracts, love expands. Guilt burdens, forgiveness liberates. When we hold onto anger, we create inflammation. When we live in fear, we suppress immunity. Conversely, when we cultivate joy, peace, and trust, we activate healing responses.

Awareness is the first medicine.

2. The Language of the Body

Our bodies speak to us—not in words, but through discomfort, tension, and illness. Each part of the body holds symbolic meaning: Throat issues may reflect unspoken truth or suppressed creativity. Heart problems may indicate unresolved grief or lack of self-love. Lower back pain might symbolize financial insecurity or lack of support. Instead of seeing illness as a punishment, we can see it as a message, inviting us to listen more deeply and love ourselves more fully.

3. Thoughts That Heal vs. Thoughts That Harm

Negative thought patterns—self-criticism, blame, unworthiness—act like slow poisons to the spirit and body. They become the internal script that influences behavior, relationships, and health.

To heal, we must rewrite the story we tell ourselves. Replace:

- "I'm not good enough" with "I am enough, just as I am."
- "Nothing ever works out" with "Life supports me in every possible way."
- "I always get sick" with "I am vibrant, whole, and thriving."

These affirmations are not fantasies—they are new energetic pathways that reshape both mind and matter.

4. *Emotional Alchemy: Forgiveness and Letting Go*

Healing requires the release of old wounds. Holding onto resentment, shame, or guilt is like drinking poison and expecting someone else to suffer. Forgiveness is not condoning the hurt—it is freeing yourself from the burden.
Practice:

- 1. Sit quietly, breathing deeply.
- 2. Visualize the person or situation that hurt you.
- 3. Say silently: "I forgive you, I release you, I set myself free."
- 4. Feel the emotional weight lifting.

This is not a one-time act—it is a healing ritual that may need repetition

5. Reclaiming Self-Love

At the core of all true healing is self-love. Not vanity, but a deep appreciation for your own worth, a tender respect for your needs, and a willingness to nurture yourself as you would a beloved child.
Ways to cultivate self-love:

- Speak kindly to yourself.
- Nourish your body with good food, rest, and movement.
- Surround yourself with beauty and positivity.
- Set boundaries with compassion and clarity.
- You cannot pour from an empty cup. Fill yours first.

6. Healing Affirmation Ritual

A daily healing affirmation practice can rewire your inner world and transform your outer life.

<u>Daily Ritual:</u>

Stand before a mirror. Look into your eyes. Speak affirmations with sincerity, such as: "I am willing to change" ,"I love and accept myself exactly as I am", "Every cell in my body is radiant with health."

7. The Inner Commitment to Heal

Healing is not linear. It is a spiral journey that may revisit old wounds, test your patience, and challenge your beliefs. But if you remain committed, with compassion and consistency, you will emerge transformed. Healing is not about becoming someone else—it's about returning to who you truly are: a whole, radiant, loving being.

Conclusion

You are not broken. You do not need to be fixed. You only need to return to love—to clear the debris of old beliefs and emotional scars, and allow your natural state of well-being to shine through. Healing is not found outside—it begins within, in the quiet moments of truth, self-compassion, and unwavering faith in your inner light.

VI

Posture, Speech, and Expression

According to ancient Vedic wisdom—as emphasized by Prash Trivedi—our body, voice, and face are not random expressions of personality. They are manifestations of cosmic intelligence, shaped by the influence of the Navagrahas (nine planets) and the gunas (sattva, rajas, tamas) that govern nature.

Every movement, word, and glance is a transmission of energy. When our posture collapses, our speech becomes reckless, or our face tightens with unconscious emotion, we distort the signal. But when we learn to center these three aspects, we restore inner alignment and reconnect with the spiritual grid.

1. The Sacred Geometry of Posture

Prash Trivedi often refers to the human body as a microcosm of the cosmos, where the spine is Mount

Meru—the energetic axis connecting Earth (Muladhara) and Heaven (Sahasrara). A centered posture is not cosmetic. It is a structural necessity for spiritual integrity.

Practice:

- Sit or stand with the crown lifted and tailbone grounded.
- Ensure ears, shoulders, hips, and heels are in alignment.
- Feel a subtle upward pull, balanced by a downward grounding.

Poor posture bends your field, like a crooked antenna. A straight spine allows your inner signal to rise and harmonize with the universal current.

2. The Power of Speech

Vak Shakti In the Vedic tradition, Vak (speech) is not just communication; it is creative force. Every syllable is encoded with mantric power and planetary resonance. Trivedi links the Mercury principle to how we speak and interpret meaning. A misused tongue is not just impolite—it generates energetic karma.

Qualities of Centred Speech:

- Sattvic: truthful, kind, measured.
- Rajasik: boastful, reactive, manipulative.
- Tamasik: harsh, cynical, destructive.

Technique: Practice pause before speech—let your words rise from silence. Tone and vibrational clarity matter more than content. Use seed mantras (e.g., Ham for Vishuddhi chakra) to tune your voice.

3. The Mirror of the Face – Emotional Yantra

Your facial expressions broadcast your subtle field. Chronic tension in the face leaks energy, confuses others' intuition, and disrupts astral cohesion.

4. Triadic Integration: The Embodied Yogi

When posture, speech, and expression harmonize, you become a living mandala—a pattern of coherence.

When in alignment:

- Your presence becomes magnetic.
- Your words carry conviction and compassion.
- Your gaze comforts or awakens those around you.

When misaligned:

- The body sags under unconscious habits.
- Speech becomes a source of confusion or harm.
- The face transmits misaligned vibrations, affecting your aura.

As Prash Trivedi writes, these distortions are not "bad"—they are clues to deeper imbalance, often astrologically or karmically rooted. Awareness begins the correction.

5. Daily Alignment Ritual

Morning Practice (5–7 minutes):
    Step 1 – Posture Reset

- Stand tall or sit in Siddhasana.
- Visualize a golden thread pulling your crown up, and roots growing from your feet.

    Step 2 – Vocal Purification

- Chant the seed sound "Ham" 7 times.
- Recite: "My words are sacred. My voice is clear. My truth is kind."

    Step 3 – Facial Presence

- Gaze into a mirror with softness.
- Release the jaw.
- Breathe into the forehead. Smile slightly.
- Practice inner stillness of the face.

Conclusion

To master your body, voice, and face is not vanity—it is vibration management. These are the instruments of your karma, and when played with awareness, they become tools of liberation. As Trivedi reminds us through the Vedic lens, we are living symbols, always in dialogue with the cosmos. In a world of distortion and noise, the centered individual becomes a transmitter of light, peace, and harmony. Alignment is not perfection—it is intention made visible. Let your posture, speech, and face reflect the divinity you already are.

VII

Vipassana- The Art of Seeing Things as They Are

In a world overflowing with stimulation and distraction, Vipassana meditation offers a return to simplicity—a journey inward through stillness, silence, and pure observation. Rooted in the teachings of Gautama the Buddha, Vipassana means "to see clearly" or "insight". It is not about controlling the mind but witnessing the truth of experience without reaction.

Unlike methods that involve chanting, visualization, or control of breath, Vipassana asks you to do something radical: just observe—your body, your mind, your sensations—without interference. It is a purification through awareness.

The Essence of Vipassana

At the heart of Vipassana lies a profound insight: everything changes. The body changes, emotions change, thoughts come and go. Nothing is permanent. This truth, called Anicca (impermanence), is not a philosophy—it is a truth you directly experience through sustained observation.

When you observe sensations without craving or aversion, you begin to liberate yourself from suffering. You see how clinging causes misery, and letting go brings peace. Vipassana doesn't promise instant bliss—it promises freedom, clarity, and deep-rooted transformation.

The Technique – A Step-by-Step Guide

1.Preparation: Cultivating Awareness through Anapana

Before diving into body sensation, you begin by sharpening awareness through Anapana, the observation of natural breath. Sit in a quiet space with spine straight and body relaxed. Focus your attention on the tip of the nose. Observe the natural breath as it flows in and out. Don't manipulate the breath—just feel it. **Purpose**: This stage stabilizes the mind and prepares it for deeper observation. Practice Anapana for 10–15 minutes daily before moving into Vipassana.

2. Vipassana Proper: Scanning the Body

Once the mind is somewhat focused, you begin to observe bodily sensations without labeling or reacting. Slowly shift attention through the body from head to feet and feet to head. Wherever you place attention, observe sensations—tingling, pressure, heat, pain, or even numbness. Do not crave pleasant sensations or reject unpleasant ones. Just observe and move on.

Golden Rule: "Remain equanimous—no matter what you feel." In doing so, you decondition the mind's habit of reacting, and begin releasing deep-rooted mental patterns (called sankharas).

Why Silence? Why Stillness?

In traditional retreats, noble silence (mauna) is observed—not just of speech but of gestures and eye contact. This creates a container where the unconscious patterns of mind rise to the surface. Stillness allows us to face ourselves. And in that confrontation, healing begins.

Benefits of Vipassana

- Mental Clarity: Sharpens attention and dissolves confusion.
- Emotional Healing: Releases suppressed traumas without analysis.
- Spiritual Insight: Reveals the truth of existence beyond the ego.
- Compassion: As self-attachment dissolves, universal love arises.

The Path of Inner Alchemy

Vipassana is not a technique for escapism. It is a spiritual alchemy, dissolving illusions and conditioning. In the furnace of silence, you meet your restlessness, your fear, your craving—and transcend them by seeing them clearly. As Goenka Ji, one of the foremost modern teachers of

Vipassana, said: > "Vipassana is the art of living. Not escaping, but living with full awareness."

Conclusion

Vipassana is a return to the essence—the unfiltered experience of the present moment. No mantra, no idol, no visualization. Just you, your body, your breath, and your sensations—all observed in silence. In the stillness of observation, you reclaim your energy. In the space between sensations, you rediscover the timeless, changeless awareness behind all phenomena.

VIII

The Spiritual and Ethical Laws

Nature operates in silence, precision, and harmony. The sun rises without command, rivers flow without rebellion, trees give without condition. Hidden within these movements are spiritual and ethical laws—not man-made rules, but cosmic principles that govern both the external universe and the inner life of the soul. These laws are not enforced—they are observed. Those who align with them move in rhythm with existence. Those who violate them, consciously or not, face imbalance, suffering, or stagnation. To walk the spiritual path is to learn to live in tune with these deeper laws, not merely by reading them, but by experiencing them within.

1. The Law of Cause and Effect (Karma)

"As you sow, so shall you reap." This is not a moral command—it is a law of energetic resonance. Every thought, emotion, word, and action sends out a vibration that returns to the source. Karma is not punishment—it is precision. Speak with hatred, and hatred returns. Act with generosity, and abundance flows back. Just as gravity pulls all objects to the earth, karma pulls all intentions back to the self. Understanding this law cultivates responsibility, mindfulness, and compassion.

2. The Law of Balance (Dharma)

Dharma is not merely duty—it is cosmic alignment. Each being has a natural function, just as each element has its role: air moves, fire transforms, water purifies. To live in dharma means: Acting according to your higher nature. Speaking truth when needed. Expressing power with humility. Choosing peace over ego. When you go against your dharma—your truth—you feel conflict. When you live in it, there is flow, synchronicity, and inner peace.

3. The Law of Harmony (Ahimsa)

Ahimsa, often translated as non-violence, is more than abstaining from harm—it is living in harmony with all life. It invites you to: Let go of mental aggression. Refrain from hurting others through speech or judgment. Cultivate kindness, even in silence. Ahimsa doesn't mean weakness—it is strength rooted in love. Like the ocean that calmly holds all storms, the practitioner of ahimsa becomes a sanctuary for peace.

4. The Law of Truth (Satya)

Truth is not just honesty—it is alignment with reality. Truth exists beyond opinion, belief, or emotion. Satya requires clarity in thought. Satya demands integrity in action. Satya offers liberation when lived from within. When you speak or act from your authentic center, you align with satya. The universe supports those who uphold truth—not out of favor, but through natural resonance.

5. The Law of Impermanence (Anicca)

Everything in nature changes—seasons, bodies, emotions, relationships. This law teaches that clinging is the root of suffering. Recognizing impermanence brings: Detachment without apathy. Gratitude for the present. Courage to release what no longer serves. Like leaves falling in autumn, letting go is not loss—it is making space for rebirth.

6. The Law of Reflection (Inner = Outer)

The world you see is a mirror of your inner state. If your mind is agitated, even the breeze feels harsh. If your heart is open, even silence feels like music. This law teaches: change within, and the world around you shifts. Anger outside? Examine inner resentment. Chaos outside? Observe internal clutter. Peace outside? It often mirrors your surrender. This reflection is not punishment—it is guidance.

7. The Law of Service (Seva)

All of nature gives—trees offer oxygen, rivers offer water, bees pollinate flowers. This law reminds us that to serve is to evolve. True service is not sacrifice; it is expression of the soul's abundance. Serve not for approval, but out of love. Help not to save, but to share light. Give not to earn karma, but because you are karma in motion. The one who serves uplifts both self and world.

• 34 •

Conclusion

These laws are not commandments carved in stone—they are truths whispered by the cosmos. When we observe the river, the moon, the silence of a mountain—we see wisdom in motion. These are not separate from us. We are made of the same laws. To walk the spiritual path is to remember what nature already knows. To return to the flow. To live by principle, not pressure. And in that remembrance, life becomes not just a journey—but a symphony.

IX

The Law of Infection - Psychological and Spiritual Contagion

Energy is contagious. Just as physical illnesses can spread through proximity, emotions, thoughts, and intentions also radiate and infect the space around us. This subtle but potent truth is known as the Law of Infection—not in a biological sense alone, but in the psychological and spiritual dimensions of our lives. You catch more than colds from those around you. You can absorb fear, doubt, anger, or alternatively courage, peace, and love—depending on who you surround yourself with, what you expose your mind to, and how open your inner field is. Recognizing this law is essential for self-mastery, energy hygiene, and spiritual growth.

1. The Psychological Dimension of Infection

Emotional Contagion

Have you ever entered a room where someone was angry, and without a word, felt the tension rise in your own body? Or perhaps laughed uncontrollably just because someone else was laughing? These are examples of emotional contagion.

- Emotions are energetic vibrations.
- Human beings, with their mirror neurons, subconsciously sync with others.
- Prolonged exposure can rewire your mental-emotional patterns.

Thus, spending time with anxious or cynical people can make you anxious or cynical—even without realizing it.

Quote: "You are the average of the five people you spend the most time with." – Jim Rohn

Just like viral misinformation can infect a digital system, toxic thought patterns—complaining, blaming, self-pity—can spread among groups, creating collective dysfunction. Gossip, pessimism, and fear can take root in the subconscious if not consciously filtered. Your mind is fertile soil. Choose carefully what you let be planted.

2. The Spiritual Dimension of Infection

Energy Fields Interact

Spiritual traditions around the world recognize that each individual carries an energetic field or aura, which reflects their current state of consciousness. An agitated person emits a chaotic field. A calm, meditative being emits a harmonious field. When fields interact, the stronger or more dominant one often influences the weaker. This is why spending time with evolved souls or in sacred spaces naturally uplifts one's state. On the other hand, being around dark, manipulative, or unconscious energies can cloud your clarity, drain your prana, or distort your inner compass.

Vibrational Influence

Energy knows no boundaries. Just as radio waves travel invisibly and influence devices, thought forms and intentions silently influence consciousness. Prayers uplift others across distance. Envy and hate can disturb the targeted mind—if it's unguarded.

3. Protection and Purification

Understanding the Law of Infection calls for psychic hygiene and conscious living.

Ways to Protect Your Inner Field:

- Conscious Association: Choose company that uplifts, rather than depletes you.
- Daily Energy Cleansing: Through meditation, grounding, breathwork, or salt baths.

- Sacred Boundaries: Learn to say no without guilt. Protect your space.
- Inner Stability: The stronger your inner anchor, the less you're influenced by outer waves.
-

Transmutation, Not Rejection

Avoiding all negativity is unrealistic. The higher way is to transmute it: Meet anger with presence. Respond to gossip with silence. Counter fear with calm.

4. *The Teacher Within Infection*

The Law of Infection also reveals what's still vulnerable within us. If another's anger triggers your rage, it reveals unhealed wounds. If envy arises when you see another succeed, it points to hidden insecurity. Infection shows us where we are not yet immune. By facing it consciously, we grow.

Conclusion

The Law of Infection is not to be feared—but to be respected. Just as you wash your body and mind daily, cleanse your energy and environment too.

Remember: You are not only vulnerable to infection—you are also a source of it. Your peace can spread like fire. Your smile can shift a room. Your silence can anchor chaos. By keeping your inner space sacred and choosing your vibrations wisely, you become not just protected—but protective—a lighthouse in a world often lost in storm.

X

The Harmony Within: Brain-Heart Coherence

We live in a culture that glorifies the intellect, where decisions are weighed in logic, outcomes, and data. Yet beneath this analytical layer, our heart pulses not just with blood—but with wisdom. The ancient mystics and modern scientists are beginning to agree on one profound truth: true intelligence arises when the brain and heart are in harmony.

This synergy is called brain–heart coherence—a state where the mind and the emotional center work in unison, producing clarity, emotional balance, creativity, and inner alignment.

The Science Behind the Coherence

The heart is more than a pump. It has its own complex nervous system, often referred to as the heart-brain, which can sense, feel, learn, and remember. It sends far more information to the brain than it receives. These signals influence:

- Cognitive functions
- Perception
- Emotional regulation

When the rhythms of the heart are smooth and ordered, the brain synchronizes with this rhythm. This state of coherence results in optimized brain function, enhanced decision-making, and reduced stress. This is not mystical speculation—it's measurable. Organizations like the HeartMath Institute have demonstrated that emotions like gratitude, compassion, and love immediately induce coherence between heart and brain rhythms.

The Spiritual Dimension

From the spiritual lens, brain–heart coherence is the alignment of reason with intuition, logic with love, intellect with soul. The brain thinks. The heart knows. When coherence is achieved, your choices are no longer reactive—they are responsive and wise. You begin to act from your center, rather than from past conditioning or fear. In moments of silence, prayer, or deep presence, we often feel this alignment—where the chatter of the mind softens, and the guidance of the heart becomes clear.

Symptoms of Incoherence

- Mental fog or confusion
- Emotional reactivity or numbness
- Indecisiveness and overthinking
- Inner conflict or chronic stress
- Feeling disconnected from one's deeper self

This dissonance leads to poor decision-making and energetic exhaustion.

Practice to cultivate coherence

1. Heart-Focused Breathing Technique:

- Sit in a quiet place. Close your eyes.
- Begin to breathe slowly and deeply, and bring your awareness to the area around your heart.
- Imagine each breath flowing in and out of the heart space.
- Do this for 2–5 minutes. This simple practice begins to synchronize heart and brain rhythms

2. Emotional Shift (Elevated Emotions)

While doing heart-breathing, gently bring into awareness a memory or feeling of gratitude, love, compassion, or peace. Let the emotion expand in your chest. This activates a biological state of coherence—a wave of electromagnetic balance through your system.

3. Coherent Listening and Speaking

- First connect with your heart.
- Maintain inner calm and stillness.
- Speak from a place of grounded truth and care.

This transforms communication into a healing field and aligns your mind-body energy.

4. Nature Immersion

The natural world operates in coherence. Trees, rivers, and skies are in constant silent alignment. Spending time in nature entrains your body into its rhythm, making coherence easier to access.

Signs of Coherence

- Stillness and alertness at once
- A sense of flow in speech and thought
- Calm confidence, even under pressure
- A felt sense of "rightness" in decisions
- Physical ease and emotional clarity

Conclusion

In a world filled with mental noise and emotional overstimulation, brain–heart coherence is not a luxury—it is a necessity. It is the gateway to presence, intuition, and self-mastery. When your mind listens to the wisdom of your heart, your life becomes a reflection of both clarity and compassion. Let this alignment be your inner compass. In that still space where brain and heart meet, you'll find not just balance—but the beginning of true transformation

XI

Tratak

In the realm of yogic sciences, there exists a practice so subtle and yet so transformative that it requires no tools, chants, or rituals—just a single black dot and the disciplined gaze of the seeker. This is Dot Tratak, a simple but profound technique to train the mind through the eyes and awaken inner perception.

Dot Tratak (Bindu Trataka in Sanskrit) is the practice of focusing one's gaze on a small black dot on a white background. It purifies the eyes, steadies the mind, and activates the Ajna chakra, the center of inner wisdom.

--- Why the Dot?

The black dot is a symbol of oneness, infinity, and the source from which all form arises. Unlike dynamic objects like candle flames, the dot does not flicker. It is stillness embodied, encouraging the mind to mirror that same state. Focusing on the dot also removes visual noise, which in turn minimizes mental noise. With practice, the practitioner learns to enter silence through the portal of the gaze.

Benefits of Dot Tratak

1. Sharpens Concentration – The practice refines the mind into a single-pointed instrument.

2. Purifies Vision – It exercises and strengthens the eye muscles, aiding visual health.

3. Activates the Third Eye – Stimulates the Ajna chakra, enhancing clarity, intuition, and selfawareness.

4. Calms Mental Fluctuations – Helps in overcoming anxiety, overthinking, and restlessness.

5. Deepens Meditation – Prepares the mind for Dharana and Dhyana by removing mental distractions.

How to Practice Dot Tratak (Bindu Trataka) What You'll Need: A small black dot (about 1–1.5 cm diameter) on a plain white paper or wall A quiet, dimly lit room A steady, comfortable seat (like Sukhasana)

1. Prepare the Space

Paste the paper with the dot on a wall at eye level, around 3–4 feet away. Ensure the room is silent and the light is soft—not too bright.

2. Sit in Stillness

Sit cross-legged with your spine erect. Place your hands on your knees in Chin or Gyan Mudra. Breathe deeply and settle your body.

3. Begin the Gaze Open your eyes and fix them softly on the black dot. Do not strain or squint. Keep your face relaxed. Try not to blink, but do not force it—allow natural

blinking if needed.

4. When Eyes Water or Blink

Gently close your eyes and observe the afterimage of the dot in your mind's eye. Keep your awareness on this inner image until it fades.

5. Repeat Reopen the eyes and return to the dot. Repeat the cycle for 5–10 minutes in the beginning, slowly increasing over time.

6. Close with Integration After your final round, rub your palms together to generate warmth. Cup them over your closed eyes. Rest and absorb the sensations in silence for a few moments.

Subtle Techniques to Enhance Tratak

Ajna Awareness: While gazing, also gently place your attention on the space between your eyebrows.

Breath Synchronization: Maintain calm, rhythmic breathing to deepen stillness.

Internal Mantra (Optional): Mentally repeat a simple mantra like "So-Ham" or "Om" if the mind wanders. ---

Precautions

Avoid if you have serious eye issues or are recovering from eye surgery.

Do not strain or extend the practice beyond comfort, especially in the beginning.

Practice in moderation—quality over duration.

Spiritual Insight

In yogic psychology, the black dot represents the bindu, or seed of creation. When one gazes steadily upon it, inner chaos dissolves, and the light behind the mind begins to glow. The practitioner eventually perceives that the dot is not out there—it is within.

As the gaze becomes pure, so does the thought. And in the moment when the dot disappears and the mind becomes empty, pure awareness dawns.

Conclusion

Dot Tratak is a deceptively simple technique with profound impact. In a world fragmented by noise and overstimulation, this practice brings back the power of singular focus. Through the art of gazing at nothing, we begin to see everything.

XII

Understanding the Circadian Clock

There is a divine order woven into the very fabric of life—a rhythm that echoes through every living being on Earth. This rhythm, known as the circadian cycle, is not merely biological; it is sacred. Like the pulse of the universe, it guides our wakefulness, our rest, and even our emotions, anchoring us to the cosmic dance of day and night.

The Inner Clock

At the core of our brain, nestled within the hypothalamus, lies the suprachiasmatic nucleus (SCN)—the master clock. This tiny bundle of neurons responds to light, syncing our internal world with the external environment. It dictates when we sleep, rise, eat, and release hormones. It is the hidden conductor orchestrating the symphony of life within us.

But the circadian rhythm is not confined to science alone—it is the architecture of harmony. The Vedas speak of Brahma Muhurta, a sacred time just before dawn, when the body and mind are most attuned to spiritual pursuits. This wisdom aligns beautifully with what modern chronobiology confirms: the hours before sunrise are a peak window for clarity, focus, and inner alignment.

Light: The Sacred Trigger

Light is not just illumination; it is communication. Morning sunlight tells our SCN that it's time to awaken. The hormones follow suit—cortisol rises to energize us, while melatonin, the sleep hormone, retreats. In the evening, darkness signals the reverse. This cycle is sacred because it keeps us aligned with nature, with the Earth's rotation and the universe's precision.

When we defy this rhythm—staying up late under artificial light, ignoring sunrise, or eating at odd hours—we fall out of sync. Fatigue, anxiety, depression, and even chronic illness can follow. Disconnection from the circadian rhythm is disconnection from life's intelligent design.

The Divine Blueprint

The ancients did not need scientific instruments to understand this rhythm. Yogic traditions emphasized waking before the sun, eating during daylight, and sleeping under starlight. Temples rang bells at dawn and dusk—not just for ritual, but to reset the inner clocks of devotees. These practices were not superstition; they were alignment with a deeper cosmic code.

The circadian rhythm is not merely about sleep—it is about energy, immunity, clarity, and consciousness. When we respect it, we tap into a wellspring of vitality. Our intuition sharpens. Our creativity flows. Our emotions find balance.

Reclaiming the Sacred Rhythm

To honor this rhythm is to honor life itself. Here's how we begin:

Rise with the Sun: Wake between 4–6 AM. Let the first light enter your eyes and skin—this resets your internal clock.

Eat with Awareness: Consume your largest meals when the sun is high. Digestive fire, or agni, is strongest then.

Disconnect Before Dusk: Dim lights after sunset. Avoid screens that emit blue light, which confuses your brain into thinking it's still daytime.

Sleep by 10 PM: This allows you to enter deep restorative sleep phases aligned with hormonal cycles.

Observe Silence at Dawn and Dusk: These are spiritual portals—times when the veil between the seen and unseen thins.

Final Thought

The circadian rhythm is not just biology. It is the Sacred Code hidden in your body—your link to the celestial intelligence that governs all life. When you return to this rhythm, you return to yourself. To live in harmony with it is not only wise—it is holy.

XIII

The symphony of Thought- Brain waves

The human mind is not merely a collection of thoughts; it is a field of vibration, a river of subtle energy constantly flowing through frequencies. Just as a musical instrument plays different notes, our brain emits different waves—each representing a unique state of consciousness.

These brain waves are not limited to neurological activity alone; they are bridges between the body, mind, and soul. Understanding them helps us live with greater awareness, inner clarity, and spiritual harmony.

The Five Frequencies of the Human Mind

Modern science classifies brain waves into five primary categories, each linked with specific states of being. From a spiritual perspective, these are not just mechanical patterns but sacred rhythms of consciousness.

1. Beta Waves (12–40 Hz): The Mind in Action

Beta is the frequency of alertness, logic, analysis, and problem-solving.

It is dominant in our waking hours when we interact with the outer world.

Spiritual View: While useful, an excess of Beta can lead to overthinking, stress, and disconnection from the inner self.

2. Alpha Waves (8–12 Hz): The Peaceful Mind

Alpha waves arise during calm states—light meditation, daydreaming, and creative thought.

The mind becomes quiet, yet alert.

Spiritual View: Alpha is the threshold between the conscious and the subconscious. It is ideal for introspection, prayer, and connecting to the heart's wisdom.

3. Theta Waves (4–8 Hz): The Gateway Within

Theta is the frequency of deep meditation, dreams, and inner vision.

It occurs in the moments between sleep and wakefulness, or during deep spiritual practice.

Spiritual View: In this state, the mind turns inward. Intuition awakens. Emotional healing and inner guidance arise effortlessly.

4. Delta Waves (0.5–4 Hz): The State of Deep Stillness

Delta is found in deep, dreamless sleep and in the deepest states of meditation.

Spiritual View: This is the silence beneath all thought. In this sacred space, the soul rests in the Divine, beyond words, beyond form.

5. Gamma Waves (40+ Hz): The Light of Awareness

Gamma waves are linked with moments of deep insight, compassion, and spiritual awakening.

Spiritual View: This is the radiant clarity found in advanced meditation or spontaneous revelations. It reflects the oneness of being and heightened perception.

Brain Waves and the Inner Path

Every spiritual tradition, knowingly or unknowingly, engages with brain waves through practice:

Breathwork (Prānāyāma) regulates energy flow, calming the mind from Beta to Alpha.

Mantra japa refines mental patterns and awakens Theta and Gamma states.

Meditation (Dhyāna) slows the mental current, moving the practitioner into the serenity of Alpha and Theta, sometimes even Delta.

Silence (Mauna) and conscious presence harmonize brain activity and allow the deeper self to shine through.

By aligning our brain waves with our intentions, we purify the mind and attune ourselves to subtle truth. This alignment is the foundation of inner peace, wisdom, and clarity.

Harmonizing the Mind Naturally

A few simple ways to balance brain wave activity:

Morning sunlight and nature walks support natural Beta-Alpha transitions.

Daily meditation opens the Theta gateway and promotes emotional harmony.

Listening to sacred music or natural sounds induces Alpha and Theta rhythms.

Sleep hygiene supports healthy Delta activity, allowing the body and mind to rejuvenate.

Final Reflection

The mind is not an enemy to be conquered, but a sacred instrument to be tuned. Brain waves are the strings of this inner instrument. When played with awareness, they produce the music of balance, clarity, and joy.

Mastering these rhythms is not a matter of control, but of awareness. As we align with our natural states of consciousness, we become more peaceful, more insightful, and more in harmony with the divine rhythm of life itself.

XIV

The Power of Pranayama

The breath is more than just a function of survival—it is the thread that connects body, mind, and spirit. Across ancient systems of knowledge, the breath was revered as a carrier of prana—the subtle life energy that fuels all aspects of our being.

Pranayama, the conscious regulation of breath, is the art of channeling this inner energy to awaken vitality, focus, and inner peace. With dedicated practice, it becomes a powerful tool to purify the system, enhance clarity, and center the self in moments of chaos.

This chapter introduces eight transformative pranayama techniques, each with its own unique benefit and purpose.

The Eight Pranayama Techniques

These breathwork exercises are suitable for anyone with basic breath awareness. As always, practice gently, on an empty stomach, and never force or strain the breath. Consistency matters more than intensity.

1. Nadi Shodhana – Alternate Nostril Breathing

Purpose: Balances the left and right energy channels, calms the mind, harmonizes emotions.

How to Practice:

Sit comfortably with your spine upright.
Close your right nostril with your right thumb.
Inhale slowly through the left nostril.
Close the left nostril with your ring finger, release the right.
Exhale through the right nostril.
Inhale through the right, switch, and exhale through the left.
Duration: 5–10 minutes daily.
Benefits: Mental clarity, stress relief, energetic balance.

2. Bhastrika – Bellows Breath

Purpose: Rapidly energizes the body and clears mental dullness.
How to Practice:
Sit upright, take a deep inhale.
Exhale forcefully through the nose.
Immediately inhale with equal force.
Repeat rapidly for 10–20 rounds.

Rest and repeat for 3–5 rounds.

Benefits: Boosts oxygenation, increases alertness, strengthens the lungs.

3. Kapalabhati – Skull-Shining Breath

Purpose: Clears stagnant energy, strengthens digestion and inner fire.

How to Practice:

Passive inhale, followed by a quick, sharp exhale from the nose, using the abdominal muscles.

Perform 20–30 short bursts, then rest.

Repeat for 3 rounds.

Benefits: Detoxifies, stimulates metabolism, awakens the mind.

Avoid if you have high blood pressure or are pregnant.

4. Ujjayi – Ocean Breath

Purpose: Builds inner heat, focuses the mind, deepens concentration.

How to Practice:

Inhale deeply through the nose while slightly constricting the throat, producing a whispering sound.

Exhale slowly with the same constriction.

Focus on the audible breath.

Duration: 5–10 minutes, especially during meditation or yoga.

Benefits: Builds willpower, reduces anxiety, enhances presence.

5. Anulom Vilom – Rhythmic Nostril Breathing

Purpose: Strengthens the nervous system, purifies energy channels.

How to Practice:

Inhale through the left nostril for a count of 4.

Retain the breath for 4 or more counts.

Exhale through the right for 4.

Repeat, alternating nostrils.

This differs from Nadi Shodhana by incorporating breath retention (Kumbhaka).

Benefits: Deepens calm, improves oxygen retention, builds focus.

6. Bhramari – Humming Bee Breath

Purpose: Relieves anxiety, improves sleep, clears mental chatter.

How to Practice:

Inhale deeply through the nose.

Exhale while making a low humming sound like a bee.

Optionally, close your eyes and gently press fingers against the ears to deepen internal focus.

Repeat for 5–10 rounds.

Benefits: Induces tranquility, supports emotional healing.

7. Surya Bhedana – Right Nostril Breathing

Purpose: Awakens the system, generates internal heat, enhances clarity.

How to Practice:

Close the left nostril.

Inhale slowly through the right nostril only.

Close both nostrils and retain the breath briefly.

Exhale through the left nostril.

Repeat for 5–10 rounds.

Benefits: Stimulates digestion, improves alertness, increases vitality.

8. Chandra Bhedana – Left Nostril Breathing

Purpose: Cools the system, calms emotional agitation, soothes the body.

How to Practice:

Close the right nostril.

Inhale through the left nostril.

Retain breath briefly.

Exhale through the right nostril.

Repeat for 5–10 rounds.

Benefits: Reduces heat, supports restful sleep, balances mood swings.

Daily Practice Suggestions

Here is a sample routine for beginners:

Time of DayPracticeDuration

MorningKapalabhati + Bhastrika + Nadi Shodhana10–15 minutes

Midday (Optional)Surya Bhedana or Ujjayi5 minutes

EveningBhramari + Chandra Bhedana + Nadi Shodhana10–15 minutes

Precautions

Always practice on an empty stomach.

Avoid holding the breath if you have heart issues, high blood pressure, or are pregnant—unless cleared by a medical professional.

Never strain; the breath should feel nourishing, not exhausting.

Start slowly and gradually increase your practice.

Conclusion: The Breath as Inner Mastery

These eight pranayama techniques offer a complete spectrum of breath-based healing and empowerment. Whether you seek vitality, calm, clarity, or emotional stability, the breath is your most intimate guide. Mastering the breath is mastering life itself.

In every inhale, we receive; in every exhale, we release. With discipline and care, this sacred exchange becomes a transformative ritual—one that awakens the deeper intelligence within.

XV
Align your Chakras

Throughout history, sound has been used to heal, focus the mind, and awaken inner power. Whether through music, mantra, or vibration, certain frequencies resonate deeply within us—restoring harmony where there was once stress or imbalance.

One of the most profound uses of sound lies in chakra chanting—the practice of using specific sounds to activate and align the body's natural energy centers. Each sound carries a vibrational signature that corresponds to a chakra. When chanted mindfully, these tones can dissolve energetic blockages, increase vitality, and foster emotional balance.

This chapter explores a simple, effective system of chakra chanting, designed to strengthen the whole self—physically, mentally, and energetically.

What Are Chakras?

In many ancient systems of health and self-mastery, chakras are seen as energy centers located along the spine, each governing different aspects of our physical body and inner life. They act like wheels or vortices, receiving, processing, and transmitting energy.

There are seven primary chakras, each linked to particular physical organs, emotional patterns, and psychological traits.

Balanced chakras allow life energy to flow freely, resulting in greater health, clarity, and connection. Chanting is one of the most effective tools to activate and harmonize these centers.

The Power of Vibration

Each chakra responds to specific vibrational frequencies. Chanting these vibrations out loud causes a resonant effect in the corresponding part of the body. Over time, this can:

Clear energetic blockages

Improve concentration and emotional health

Deepen meditation

Build a stronger sense of self-awareness and presence

Even without belief in energy systems, many people find that chanting improves mood, posture, breathing, and nervous system regulation.

Chakra Chanting Overview

Below is a simple structure for working with the chakras using vibrational syllables. These sounds are not religious mantras, but pure phonetic tones selected for their resonance.

Each sound should be drawn out slowly during the exhale. Example: If chanting "LAM," it would sound like "Laaaaaammmm..." while feeling the vibration in the associated region.

1. Root Chakra (Base of the spine)

Name: Root / Base
   Energy: Grounding, survival, physical strength
   Sound: "LAM" (pronounced "lahm")
   Vibration Area: Pelvic floor, tailbone
   Chanting Benefits: Increases stability, confidence, and presence

2. Sacral Chakra (Below the navel)

Name: Sacral
   Energy: Creativity, sensuality, emotional flow
   Sound: "VAM" (pronounced "vahm")
   Vibration Area: Lower abdomen
   Chanting Benefits: Enhances emotional intelligence, passion, fluidity

3. Solar Plexus Chakra (Stomach area)

Name: Solar Plexus
   Energy: Willpower, identity, self-mastery
   Sound: "RAM" (pronounced "rahm")
   Vibration Area: Mid-abdomen, diaphragm
   Chanting Benefits: Builds confidence, determination, personal power

4. Heart Chakra (Center of the chest)

Name: Heart
   Energy: Compassion, love, forgiveness
   Sound: "YAM" (pronounced "yahm")
   Vibration Area: Chest, heart

Chanting Benefits: Heals emotional wounds, strengthens empathy

5. Throat Chakra (Throat and neck area)

Name: Throat

Energy: Communication, truth, self-expression
Sound: "HAM" (pronounced "hahm")
Vibration Area: Throat, vocal cords
Chanting Benefits: Enhances clarity in speech, opens honest expression

6. Third Eye Chakra (Between the eyebrows)

Name: Third Eye

Energy: Intuition, insight, mental clarity
Sound: "OM" or "AUM" (pronounced "ohm")
Vibration Area: Forehead, mind
Chanting Benefits: Sharpens intuition, improves focus and imagination

7. Crown Chakra (Top of the head)

Name: Crown

Energy: Awareness, connection, higher perspective
Sound: Silent or a high-pitched "NG" (as in "sing")
Vibration Area: Crown of head
Chanting Benefits: Opens awareness, inspires peace, inner harmony

How to Practice Chakra Chanting

Step-by-Step Routine (15–20 minutes):

Find a quiet space where you can sit comfortably with a straight spine.

Close your eyes and take a few deep breaths to center yourself.

Start from the root chakra and work your way up to the crown.

For each chakra:

Visualize the area of the body.

Imagine energy activating or light expanding in that region.

Chant the corresponding sound slowly and deeply for 3–5 breaths.

After the crown, sit in silence for a few minutes to feel the effects.

Optional Enhancements:

Use visualization (color or light in the chakra area)

Place your hands gently on each area as you chant

Incorporate background music with deep tones or binaural beats

Chakra Chanting Table (Quick Reference)

ChakraAreaSoundPurpose

RootBase of spineLAMGrounding, stability

SacralLower abdomenVAMCreativity, emotional flow

Solar PlexusStomachRAMConfidence, personal power

HeartChestYAMCompassion, love

ThroatThroatHAMExpression, truth

Third EyeBrow/ForeheadOMIntuition, mental clarity

CrownTop of headNG/SilenceAwareness, unity

Benefits of Regular Practice

Greater emotional resilience
Improved posture and breath control
Calmer nervous system
Increased self-awareness
Enhanced focus and creativity

Even if you chant only a few syllables per day, you are activating a deeper relationship with your body and mind.

Conclusion: Align Through Sound

The body is an instrument, and your voice is the key to tuning it. Chakra chanting is not about belief—it is about experience. It allows you to explore how simple vibrations affect your inner state, bringing peace, power, and balance into your daily life.

With each tone, you realign not just energy, but intention, and the way you show up in the world.

XVI

Biofeedback-Intelligence of Your Body

Introduction: The Body Is Always Speaking

Your body is not just a machine—it's a living, intelligent system constantly sending you signals. Every emotion, every thought, every posture, every breath is part of a real-time feedback loop between your inner state and your environment.

Biofeedback is the art and science of learning how to listen to those signals—not through machines or devices alone, but through heightened awareness, presence, and observation. When you become sensitive to your body's subtle messages, you gain the power to self-regulate, realign, and heal from within.

This chapter introduces biofeedback not just as a tool of science, but as a natural capacity for self-mastery, rooted in awareness of rhythm, breath, emotion, and energy.

What Is Biofeedback?

At its core, biofeedback is self-observation. It means using feedback from your body—whether it's heart rate, muscle tension, skin temperature, or even intuitive signals—to guide yourself toward balance and clarity.

In clinical settings, biofeedback involves sensors and technology to measure body responses. But the deeper layer of biofeedback is internal: it's about developing the ability to sense and interpret these signals without external instruments.

You don't need a device to know when your heart races, your breath shortens, or your jaw clenches. You feel it. The question is—do you notice it early enough to change course?

The Inner Technology: Awareness as a Feedback Tool

When you increase self-awareness, you activate your inner technology—a natural intelligence that is more precise and adaptive than any external device. This is where true biofeedback begins.

Your body is like a compass. It tells you:

When you're out of alignment (through tension, fatigue, anxiety)

When you're in flow (through energy, peace, ease)

When something or someone is draining you

When you're in harmony with your environment

Learning to read these signs means you no longer need to rely on constant external validation. You become your own guide.

Biofeedback Through Natural Elements

A powerful way to practice biofeedback is by connecting with natural elements—the sun, water, wind, and earth. Nature amplifies feedback. For example:

Walking barefoot on the ground helps you feel grounded or disconnected.

Sun exposure reveals whether your body is open or tense and shielded.

Immersion in cold or warm water reveals your stress tolerance and response.

These are not mystical ideas—they are primal, biological truths. When you reorient yourself to nature, you begin to reset your internal rhythms and uncover what is real within you.

The Breath as the Master Feedback Loop

The breath is the simplest and most immediate biofeedback tool.

When anxious, it becomes shallow and fast.

When peaceful, it becomes deep and slow.

When aligned, it becomes rhythmic, effortless, and nourishing.

By consciously observing and adjusting your breath, you begin to influence your nervous system, emotions, and even thought patterns.

Try this:

Pause and take a long, slow breath.
Now hold it for a moment.
Exhale gently, with awareness.
Notice how the body responds.
This is biofeedback in real-time.

Emotional Biofeedback: Feeling the Shift

Every emotion carries a vibrational frequency and a somatic signature.

Anger feels hot, fast, expansive.

Fear feels tight, cold, contractive.

Joy feels light, open, and radiating.

When you observe the physical changes emotions bring, you can begin to choose responses that realign you, rather than reacting unconsciously.

Biofeedback means becoming emotionally fluent: recognizing what you're feeling, where it lives in the body, and how to return to center.

Signs You're Listening to Biofeedback

You pause before reacting.

You feel early signs of stress and shift your posture or breath.

You choose what nourishes you, not what numbs you.

You sense when you're around healthy vs. draining energy.

You act from alignment, not impulse.

This is not perfection—it's presence. And presence is power.

Practical Exercises: Tuning into Biofeedback

Here are three simple, daily ways to develop your internal biofeedback skillset:

1. Stillness Scan (5 minutes)

Sit quietly and do a full-body scan.

Feel for areas of tension, heat, cold, numbness, or emotion.

Breathe into each area and simply observe without judging.

This develops awareness of subtle shifts in your internal state.

2. Sun Response Awareness

Stand in sunlight for 1–2 minutes with eyes closed.

Ask yourself: Does this feel nourishing or draining today?

How does your posture, breath, and mood shift?

This teaches you to listen to your instinctual feedback to nature.

3. Emotional Pulse Check

Throughout the day, pause and ask:

What am I feeling right now?

Where do I feel this in my body?

Is my breath shallow or full?

Would a shift in breath, movement, or environment help?

This trains emotional intelligence rooted in somatic awareness.

Biofeedback Is Not Just a Technique—It's a Lifestyle

Biofeedback is not about control. It's about coherence. It's about harmonizing your inner rhythm with truth, with nature, and with your higher instinct.

When practiced regularly, you begin to:

Sleep deeper

Speak with more authenticity

Respond to life rather than react

Trust your body's wisdom

Live in natural timing rather than artificial rhythm

You become less programmable and more present.

Final Thought: Reclaiming Your Inner Guidance System

You were born with the ability to read your body. To feel your truth. To know what's right for you in any moment. Biofeedback simply reawakens that sovereign intelligence.

In a world that teaches us to outsource our knowing, biofeedback is an act of returning to your own signal. Your nervous system doesn't lie. Your breath doesn't lie. Your body doesn't lie.

When you learn to listen, you reclaim the most important connection of all—the one between you and your own truth.

XVII
Eating the Right

Introduction: Food as a Messenger

Food is not just fuel—it's information, vibration, and frequency. Every bite you take sends a message to your cells, to your energy, and to your emotions.

Most people eat for stimulation, satisfaction, or habit—not alignment. But your diet is one of the most direct ways to influence your body, mind, and longevity. And when food is chosen with awareness, it becomes a source of clarity, strength, and balance.

This chapter distills a timeless, science-backed, and nature-aligned approach to nutrition, drawing from modern research and ancient common sense—one that simplifies your relationship with food while maximizing vitality.

Why Simplicity in Diet Matters

We live in an age of over-choice and under-nourishment. Supermarkets are full of processed, artificial, and addictive products that weaken the body, cloud the mind, and create chronic inflammation.

Yet the truth is simple: the body thrives on what it was designed for—natural, whole, plant-based foods. Not supplements. Not fads. Not pills. Plants. Water. Sun-grown simplicity.

As multiple health researchers have shown, including pioneers in nutritional science, long-term health isn't built on complexity—it's built on consistency with natural law.

The Evidence Behind Plant-Based Eating

One of the most comprehensive scientific investigations into diet and health was The China Study, led by Dr. T. Colin Campbell. It found that populations who consumed predominantly whole plant foods—with very little animal protein and processed food—had the lowest rates of chronic diseases, including heart disease, cancer, and diabetes.

Key takeaways:

Animal protein, especially casein (found in dairy), was strongly linked to disease progression.

Diets rich in vegetables, fruits, grains, legumes, and greens dramatically lowered disease risk.

A return to traditional, plant-based diets helped communities live longer, healthier lives.

Food as Medicine: The Body's Natural Healing Response

Dr. B.R.C. and other health revolutionaries emphasize that disease is not an enemy—it is a feedback system. The body reacts to what you feed it. When you remove the interfering foods (processed oils, sugars, excess animal products, dairy, chemicals), the body starts to clean, repair, and regenerate.

This is not alternative medicine—this is biological common sense. Health is not created by adding more—it's created by removing the wrong inputs and returning to nature.

Core Principles of a Vital Diet

Based on decades of research, patient experience, and natural wisdom, the following principles form the core of a diet that supports healing, energy, and inner clarity.

1. Eat Whole, Unprocessed Plant Foods

Focus on foods as close to their natural state as possible: fruits, vegetables, whole grains, legumes, seeds, and leafy greens.

These foods are rich in fiber, antioxidants, minerals, and life-force energy.

Avoid anything that comes in a packet with more than five ingredients.

2. Eliminate or Minimize Animal Products

Animal protein, especially dairy and red meat, places a heavy load on digestion, kidneys, and the immune system.

Opt instead for plant proteins: lentils, chickpeas, tofu, tempeh, and leafy greens.

Transition at your own pace—but consistency is key.

3. Avoid Refined Oils and Added Sugar

Oils (even "healthy" ones) are highly processed and calorie-dense, with minimal fiber or nutrients.

Sugar spikes insulin and feeds inflammation.

Instead, eat whole fats (avocados, nuts) and sweeten naturally (dates, fruits).

4. Hydrate with Living Water

Drink pure, clean water—preferably free of chlorine and fluoride.

Add fresh lemon, herbs, or copper-vessel storage for mineral infusion.

Avoid packaged juices, soft drinks, or chemical beverages.

5. Practice Food Timing and Fasting

Give the body time to rest and repair by avoiding constant snacking.

Eat during sunlight hours (intermittent fasting helps align circadian rhythm).

A 12-14 hour nightly fast can promote detox and hormonal balance.

Simple Daily Meal Framework

Here's a daily blueprint inspired by high-vitality cultures and natural nutrition science:

? Morning (Sunrise to Midday)

Start with hydration (warm lemon water or plain water)

Fruits only in the morning (mono-meals are ideal): papaya, mango, watermelon, apple

Avoid heavy, cooked foods before noon—this supports elimination and clarity

? Afternoon (Midday to 4 PM)

Main meal of the day: steamed vegetables, whole grains (millet, brown rice), dal, lentils, greens

Optional: salad with lemon dressing or sprouts

Focus on fresh, home-cooked, colorful, and satisfying meals

? Evening (Sunset onward)

Light, warm meal if hungry: soup, boiled vegetables, herbal tea

No food after dark when possible—this allows the body to rest, digest, and regenerate overnight

Healing Happens When the Body Is Not Burdened

Dr. BRC's approach shows that the body begins to heal not through treatment, but by removing the toxic load. When digestion is light, when the food is whole and clean, the energy that was used for breakdown and inflammation now becomes available for repair and rejuvenation.

Symptoms disappear. Skin clears. Sleep deepens. Emotions stabilize.

Not because of medication, but because the conditions for healing are finally met.

Food and Mental Clarity

Diet not only affects your body—it shapes your thoughts.

Heavy, congesting foods cloud the mind.

Light, natural foods open the senses.

A whole-food, plant-based diet has been shown to:

Improve focusHeading 2

Reduce anxiety

Balance hormones

Enhance mood and emotional stability

When your inner chemistry changes, so does your outlook on life.

Common Myths, Clarified

"Where will I get my protein?"

Plant foods contain all essential amino acids. Lentils, quinoa, greens, and beans are rich sources.

"Don't we need milk for calcium?"

Leafy greens, sesame seeds, almonds, and figs are more absorbable sources of calcium than dairy.

"But it's hard to give up meat or processed food."

Change doesn't require perfection—just awareness and progress. Start small, stay consistent.

Conclusion: Eat From the Earth, Not the Factory

When you align your diet with nature and simplicity, you do more than just avoid disease—you activate life.

You begin to:

Wake up lighter

Digest easier

Think clearer

Live longer

Feel more connected to your body and the planet

You don't need a complicated diet plan or a long list of supplements.

You need real food, grown by the sun, designed by the Earth, and consumed with presence.

Eat to support life. Eat to support truth. Eat to support you.

XVIII
Power of Attention

"Where your attention goes, your energy flows."

This isn't just a quote—it's a law.

In the teachings of ancient wisdom keepers and modern sages alike, one principle stands above all: your attention determines your reality.

What you give attention to, you are literally feeding—energetically, emotionally, mentally. Whether it's people, thoughts, feelings, or frequencies—your awareness is creative.

In the world of Prashant Trivedi, attention is not just focus—it is a divine force. It is the beam of light that determines the direction of your life, your state, and your destiny.

The question is never "What's happening to me?"
The real question is, "Where is my attention going?"

The Hijacking of Human Attention

We live in a time when attention is the most harvested resource on Earth—more than oil, more than gold.

Every screen, every app, every piece of drama is designed to steal your attention—to drag it into lower vibrations, artificial thought loops, and meaningless engagement.

This is not accidental. The system depends on you feeding it with attention—because without it, it collapses.

When you give your attention to the matrix, to conflict, to fear, to artificial timelines—you are powering the very thing that disempowers you.

The most revolutionary act today is not protest or rebellion.

It is to withdraw your attention from what is false and to redirect it to what is higher.

What Is "Higher"?

When we say "give attention to the higher," we mean:

That which uplifts your vibration

That which connects you to nature, silence, and source

That which returns you to your own knowing

That which doesn't want your energy, but reflects your power back to you

The higher is not something you chase. It's already within you. But you have to tune your attention to it, like a radio signal.

When your attention is on the higher, you begin to experience:

Clarity in confusion
Strength in stillness
Guidance without seeking
Energy without stimulation
This is not theory. This is energetic physics.

Attention Shapes Frequency

Your frequency—the energetic tone of your being—is determined not by what happens to you, but by what you attend to repeatedly.

Give attention to chaos → you live in chaos.

Give attention to harmony → your body and world become harmonious.

Give attention to truth → lies start dissolving around you.

Give attention to source → you start remembering who you really are.

This is not self-help. This is sacred architecture.

Why Most People Feel Drained

It's not work. It's not others. It's not even your "problems."

It's where your attention is going.

When your attention is scattered across:

Old stories

Past pain

Toxic environments

Social comparison

Low-level entertainment
...you become energetically fragmented.

You are present, but not powerful. Awake, but not aligned.
The real solution isn't in changing the world.
It's in changing your point of attention.

Attention as Sovereignty

Prashant Trivedi teaches that your attention is your kingdom. When you give it freely to what lowers you, you're abdicating your throne.

But when you learn to protect and direct your attention, you become sovereign—untouchable by manipulation, unaffected by artificial trends, undisturbed by noise.

You become the seer, not the seen.

And from this place, you begin to live by natural law, not human programming.

How to Give Attention to the Higher

This is not about chanting mantras or thinking positive thoughts.
It's about subtle shifts in your awareness, made daily:

? 1. Return to Nature

Sit under the sun.
Watch a tree without thinking.
Walk barefoot on earth.
Give full attention to the elements. They respond.

?? 2. Observe Without Absorbing

Witness the world. Don't be consumed by it.
See what's happening, but stay anchored in yourself.
This is how you stay clean in a dirty world.

? 3. Watch Your Thoughts Like Clouds

You are not your thoughts.
Observe them as movements in the sky of your awareness.
What you don't feed, fades.

? 4. Give Attention to What Feels Real

Certain books, music, people, spaces will pull your energy up.
Others will distort, drain, or distract.
Learn the difference—not mentally, but energetically. Your body will tell you.

A Simple Practice: Attention Reset

Whenever you feel drained, anxious, or lost:
Stop.
Close your eyes.
Take three deep breaths.
Ask: "Where is my attention right now?"
Gently bring it back to your body, your breath, the sky, the now.
Even five seconds of this reset, done often, can recalibrate your frequency.

Attention Is a Doorway

You don't need more effort.
You need more precision in where your awareness goes.

Attention is the gateway to the higher realms—the natural intelligence, the inner sun, the divine law that governs everything.

If you keep looking at the ground, you will feel heavy. But if you lift your gaze—internally and externally—you begin to ascend.

You begin to rise out of confusion, out of entanglement, out of sleep.

This is what PT means when he speaks of the higher realms of being: not imagination, but a real, felt shift in awareness through the mastery of attention.

Final Thought: Your Attention Is a Gift to the Divine

You are not here to fix the world. You are here to remember what is true and be in resonance with it.

Every moment you place your attention on beauty, nature,

XIX

The DNA Phantom Effect

Introduction: Your DNA and Emotions—An Energetic Dance

Have you ever wondered why certain emotions make you feel physically different? Why joy can make you feel lighter, while anger seems to weigh you down? Or why negative emotions like fear and sadness can seem to drain your energy, affecting not just your mood but your overall well-being?

What if emotions aren't just feelings you experience in your mind—they are actually influencing your very DNA? This idea becomes even more intriguing when we consider the DNA Phantom Effect, a phenomenon that suggests DNA is not only a biological blueprint for your body but also holds energetic and informational qualities that are deeply affected by consciousness and emotions.

In this chapter, we'll explore how your emotions can shape the energetic field of your DNA, influencing not just your body's health but your overall vibration and connection to the universe.

What is DNA?

Before diving into the DNA Phantom Effect, let's first take a quick look at DNA itself. Your DNA is the blueprint for your physical body. It contains all the genetic information needed to create and maintain you as a unique individual. From your eye color to your immune system, DNA carries the instructions for your biological form.

However, recent research, including studies around the DNA Phantom Effect, has shown that DNA may have more than just a biological role. It's suggested that DNA could also hold an energetic presence—like an antenna that picks up and transmits subtle energies and frequencies, especially influenced by your consciousness and emotions.

The Phantom Effect and Your Emotions

In the 1990s, Russian scientist Pjotr Garjajev and his team conducted groundbreaking research on DNA. They discovered that DNA does not merely act as a molecular code but also appears to interact with light and energy in profound ways. They found that even after DNA was removed from the cell, it still emitted an energetic "phantom" or "ghost-like" pattern that affected its surroundings. This is what became known as the DNA Phantom Effect.

But here's the key idea: Your DNA is not just physical—it has an energetic signature, and this signature is directly affected by consciousness and emotions.

For instance, when you experience strong emotions, your body releases hormones and chemical signals that influence not only your thoughts and feelings but your DNA's energetic field. This means that your emotions have the power to change your DNA's energetic signature, affecting how it behaves and how it interacts with the world around you.

Emotions and Their Impact on Your DNA

Emotions aren't just fleeting mental states—they are powerful forces that create energetic vibrations within your body. When you experience an emotion, it is not only felt in your mind but also in your biological systems. From a scientific standpoint, emotions trigger neurotransmitters and hormones that affect your heart rate, immune system, and even the genetic expression of certain cells. This is where emotions and DNA intersect.

Here's how different emotions can impact your DNA's energetic field:

1. Positive Emotions: Light and Healing

When you feel emotions like joy, love, compassion, and gratitude, your DNA vibrates at a higher, more harmonious frequency. Positive emotions have been shown to:

Increase the flow of energy in the body, allowing cells to communicate more effectively.

Strengthen your immune system and help your body repair itself more efficiently.

Create a more open and expansive energetic field, making you more receptive to higher frequencies and universal energy.

This is when your DNA's "phantom" energy aligns with the higher frequencies of the universe, allowing you to feel more connected and empowered.

2. Negative Emotions: Blockages and Dissonance

On the other hand, when you experience negative emotions like fear, anger, shame, or sadness, your DNA's energetic field tends to contract. These emotions can cause:

Energetic blockages, disrupting the flow of energy in your body and causing dissonance in your DNA's vibration.

Lowered immunity and less effective communication between your cells.

Distorted energy patterns, which may lead to physical ailments or emotional imbalances.

These emotions create a low-frequency state in your DNA, which can make you feel disconnected from your true essence and from the world around you.

The Science Behind the Emotional Impact on DNA

So, how do emotions really affect DNA on a scientific level? It all comes down to the concept of epigenetics—the study of how environmental factors (including emotions) can turn genes on or off without altering the DNA sequence itself. Essentially, your DNA can be expressed differently based on your emotional and mental state.

When you experience positive emotions, your DNA expression can shift toward healing, vitality, and balance. Conversely, when you experience prolonged negative emotions, you might activate stress-related genes or genes linked to disease.

In addition, studies have shown that thoughts and emotions can influence the morphology of your DNA. This means that your internal state can actually reshape your genetic expression by altering the energetic frequencies around your DNA.

How to Harness Your Emotions to Heal and Strengthen Your DNA

Now that we understand the connection between emotions and DNA, the next question is: How can you consciously use your emotions to benefit your DNA?

Here are some practical steps:

1. Practice Emotional Awareness

Start by becoming aware of your emotions. Notice how different emotions feel in your body. Are they expansive and light, or tight and heavy? This awareness will help you consciously shift your emotional state when necessary.

2. Cultivate Positive Emotions

Actively seek out experiences and thoughts that make you feel joyful, loving, and grateful. Whether it's spending time with loved ones, engaging in creative activities, or simply being in nature—these positive emotions can help elevate your DNA's energetic field, allowing it to resonate with higher frequencies.

3. Release Negative Emotions

Negative emotions, when held for too long, can create blockages in your energy field. Try journaling, meditation, or breathing exercises to release pent-up negative emotions. Physical activities like yoga, running, or even just dancing can help you move the energy in your body and release it.

4. Visualization and Energy Healing

In addition to emotional regulation, you can use visualization to direct positive energy toward your DNA. Picture your DNA being bathed in golden light, and feel it vibrating at a high frequency. You can also use energy healing practices like Reiki or sound therapy to clear energetic blockages in your DNA.

5. Meditate on Unity with the Universe

Since the DNA Phantom Effect suggests that your DNA connects to a larger energetic system, you can meditate on your connection with the universe. Imagine your DNA as a bridge between your physical self and the energy fields around you. This practice can help realign your energetic field and improve your DNA's expression.

Conclusion: Your DNA and the Power of Emotion

The DNA Phantom Effect shows us that DNA is not just a physical structure but a dynamic energetic system that is influenced by our consciousness and emotions. By consciously cultivating positive emotions and releasing negative ones, we can elevate the energetic signature of our DNA, leading to greater health, vitality, and connection to the universe.

Your DNA is far more than just a biological code—it's a living, breathing energy field that responds to your thoughts, feelings, and intentions. And when you begin to understand and work with the energetic influence of your emotions, you can unlock the full potential of your DNA, leading to a more harmonious and empowered life.

XX

The Spiritual Trance State

What is a Spiritual Trance State?

Imagine a state of deep stillness, where the chatter of your mind fades away, and you are fully immersed in the present moment. A place where time seems to stand still, and you feel connected to something much larger than yourself—an inner source of wisdom, peace, and insight.

This state is known as the spiritual trance state. It is a powerful, altered state of consciousness where you can access deeper realms of your mind, uncover hidden truths, and connect with higher planes of existence. Unlike the typical waking state, a spiritual trance allows you to experience life from a non-ordinary perspective, bringing profound transformation, healing, and spiritual growth.

In this chapter, we'll explore what a spiritual trance is, how to enter this state, and the ways in which it can enhance your spiritual journey.

What is a Spiritual Trance?

A spiritual trance state is a naturally occurring altered state of consciousness, where an individual enters a deeper state of awareness that is beyond ordinary, everyday consciousness. When in this state, your connection to your higher self, the universe, or divine energy becomes stronger and clearer. It's as if you've entered into a realm where time and space lose their grip, and you are more in tune with the spiritual dimensions.

A trance state is not necessarily about losing consciousness, but rather about shifting your awareness to a different frequency, often characterized by:

Heightened sensitivity to energy: You may sense the presence of energies or beings, or experience a deeper connection to the elements of nature.

Deeper intuition: In this state, your intuition is sharpened, and you may gain insights or receive guidance from within.

Spiritual experiences: It can be a time when you receive messages, visions, or profound revelations that are not accessible in your normal waking state.

A sense of peace or bliss: Many people report feeling a profound sense of calm, peace, and oneness during trance states.

In essence, the spiritual trance state is a gateway to higher dimensions of consciousness, a place where you can tap into inner wisdom, healing, and spiritual awakening.

How to Enter a Spiritual Trance State

Entering a spiritual trance state requires both practice and intentionality. While the trance state is a natural part of the human experience, it can be deepened with focused efforts. Here are some common practices to help you enter a spiritual trance:

1. Meditation

Meditation is one of the most effective ways to enter a spiritual trance. By calming the mind and focusing your attention, you gradually release the distractions of the physical world, allowing you to connect with deeper levels of consciousness.

Breath-focused meditation: Sit in a comfortable position, close your eyes, and focus on your breath. As you breathe slowly and deeply, allow your body to relax. With each breath, imagine you are sinking deeper into a peaceful and calm state. Let go of all thoughts, and allow your mind to become still.

Guided meditation: You can also use guided meditations designed to lead you into a trance. These may include visualizations of peaceful landscapes or journeys into inner realms where spiritual insights can be received.

2. Drumming or Sound Therapy

Certain rhythmic sounds, such as drumming or the use of singing bowls, can help induce a trance state. The repetitive beats or sounds create a hypnotic effect, which helps synchronize brainwave patterns, putting you into a state of deep relaxation and heightened awareness.

Shamanic drumming: This ancient practice involves repetitive drumming to induce a trance-like state, where you may access spiritual realms or receive visions and guidance.

Sound baths: Instruments like Tibetan singing bowls or crystal bowls produce sound frequencies that resonate deeply with your body, helping you achieve a meditative trance state.

3. Breathwork

Breathwork techniques, such as holotropic breathing or pranayama (breathing exercises), are another powerful method for entering a trance state. By consciously controlling your breath, you can shift your state of consciousness and access spiritual realms.

Holotropic breathing involves rapid, deep breathing that can lead to a deep trance-like state, where you may experience emotional release, spiritual revelations, or even altered perceptions of reality.

Pranayama involves the controlled manipulation of breath, allowing you to cultivate inner energy and direct your focus, which can deepen your connection with your spiritual self.

4. Visualizations

Using visualization techniques can also guide you into a spiritual trance. By imagining peaceful or sacred images—such as a luminous light, an ancient temple, or a divine being—you can shift your focus away from the physical world and enter a trance state.

Sacred space visualization: Imagine yourself walking into a sacred space where you feel safe and connected to divine energy. In this space, you can ask for guidance, experience healing, or receive spiritual insights.

The Benefits of the Spiritual Trance State

The spiritual trance state offers many benefits, both for your personal growth and spiritual journey. Here are just a few of the powerful ways it can support your transformation:

1. Healing

A spiritual trance state can open you up to profound emotional and energetic healing. When in this altered state of consciousness, you may experience a release of old patterns or traumas that have been holding you back. This deep healing can happen on multiple levels: physical, emotional, and spiritual.

Energy clearing: You may find that in a trance state, you become more aware of blocked energy or areas of tension in your body. These areas can be released during your trance experience, allowing for healing to take place.

2. Heightened Intuition and Insight

The deeper connection to your higher self or divine wisdom that occurs in a trance state can provide you with profound insights. You may receive answers to questions you've been pondering, discover new perspectives on challenges, or receive guidance on your spiritual path.

Intuition: With your mind quieted and your awareness expanded, your intuition becomes stronger. This can be a powerful tool for personal decision-making and spiritual growth.

3. Spiritual Awakening

The trance state offers a gateway to higher states of consciousness. It can help you experience oneness with the universe, connect with spiritual guides or ancestors, and gain clarity on your purpose in life. It can lead to deep experiences of self-awareness and spiritual awakening.

Connection with the Divine: You may experience a direct connection with the divine or a higher power. This connection can foster feelings of unconditional love, peace, and purpose.

4. Manifestation and Personal Empowerment

As you enter a trance state, you align more fully with your inner power. This can significantly enhance your ability to manifest desires and create positive change in your life.

Manifestation: When you enter a deep state of awareness, your ability to visualize and manifest your desires becomes amplified. You may find that your goals and intentions are more easily realized as you operate from a space of heightened clarity and spiritual alignment.

How to Use the Spiritual Trance State for Growth and Transformation

Now that you understand what a spiritual trance state is and how to enter it, here are a few ways you can incorporate it into your daily life for personal and spiritual transformation:

1. Regular Practice

Make trance states a regular part of your practice, whether through meditation, sound therapy, or breathwork. The more you engage with these practices, the easier it will be to access deeper states of consciousness.

2. Set Intentions

Before entering a trance state, set clear intentions for what you wish to achieve. Whether you seek healing, answers to questions, or spiritual growth, your intention will guide the experience and help you stay focused.

3. Keep a Journal

After each trance experience, take time to journal your insights, visions, or emotions. Writing down your experiences can help you integrate what you've learned and track your spiritual growth over time.

4. Seek Guidance from Experienced Practitioners

If you're new to trance states, consider learning from experienced spiritual guides or shamanic practitioners who can guide you into deeper states of consciousness. Their expertise can help you navigate the experience safely and effectively.

Conclusion: Embracing the Spiritual Trance State

The spiritual trance state is a powerful tool for spiritual growth, healing, and transformation. By entering this altered state of consciousness, you can access deeper realms of wisdom, experience healing, and align more fully with your true essence. As you integrate the practices and teachings in this chapter, you will unlock new dimensions of self-awareness, empowerment, and divine connection.

May the trance state be a portal to your inner wisdom, and may it lead you to a life of deeper peace, clarity, and spiritual awakening.

SOURCES

- *Earthinginstitute.net*

- *Yoga for men only- Frank Rudolph Young*

- *You can heal your life- Louise Hay*

- *Heal your body- Louise Hay*

- *PT speaks*

- *Whale.to*

- *The China Study and Dr BRC videos*

- *CIA gateway process*

- *Joyofsatan ministry*

Researches by spiritual scientist

PMC

The 48 Laws of Power- Robert Greene